Original title:
The Midnight Magic Show

Copyright © 2024 Creative Arts Management OU
All rights reserved.

Author: Maya Livingston
ISBN HARDBACK: 978-9916-90-496-1
ISBN PAPERBACK: 978-9916-90-497-8

Dance of the Celestial Creatures

In the night sky, stars do twirl,
Moonbeams shimmer, gently swirl.
Glowing comets race with grace,
In this vast, enchanted space.

Whispers of the cosmic winds,
Through the dark, their journey spins.
Constellations weave their song,
As the universe hums along.

A ballet of the astral lights,
Flickering in endless nights.
Galaxies in radiant hues,
A wondrous dance for us to view.

As dawn approaches, they all fade,
Yet their magic never strayed.
In our hearts, their rhythm stays,
Guiding us through countless days.

Secrets of the Enchanted Hour

In twilight's glow, the secrets dwell,
Whispers of magic begin to swell.
Shadows stretch, the day concedes,
To the night and all its needs.

The air is thick with mystery,
Enchanting tales of history.
Stars appear, like eyes so bright,
Guardians of the coming night.

With every tick, the hour calls,
Underneath the moonlit walls.
Wonders rise from slumber's grace,
In this sacred, timeless space.

As dreams and reality entwine,
The heart feels fate's gentle sign.
In the folds of this twilight,
Lie the secrets of the night.

Moonlit Illusions

In the glow of silver skies,
Dreams awaken, softly rise.
Whispers dance on the cool breeze,
Guiding hearts with gentle ease.

Shadows play in the night's embrace,
Stars twinkle in their secret place.
Each moment holds a fleeting chance,
To lose ourselves in a twilight trance.

Reflections shimmer on the lake,
Mirrored whispers, what we make.
Underneath the moon's soft gaze,
We find peace in this quiet maze.

Hold my hand, let's drift away,
In the silence, let us stay.
For in this night, all is revealed,
Moonlit truths, our hearts unsealed.

Secrets Beneath the Stars

Beneath the stars, we seek the truth,
In a dance of shadows, ageless youth.
Mysteries wrapped in cosmic light,
Calling us to the depths of night.

Each twinkle holds a hidden tale,
Of lovers lost and dreams that sail.
Wishes whispered on the breeze,
Carried far with gentle ease.

The universe hums a sacred song,
In its rhythm, we all belong.
Secrets lie in the quiet dark,
Waiting for the hearts to spark.

Let us wander through this dream,
Unified in a soft moonbeam.
For in the dark, we find our goals,
Secrets unravel, revealing souls.

Enchanted Shadows

In the forest where secrets dwell,
Enchanted shadows weave their spell.
With every rustle, magic stirs,
Whispers of night, soft and blurred.

Trees sway gently to a tune,
Beneath the watchful, silver moon.
Creatures linger, hidden from sight,
In the embrace of the velvety night.

Fading paths where dreams collide,
Mystical figures shift and glide.
Every heartbeat synchronizes,
With the magic nature realizes.

Let us step where few have been,
In this world of evergreen.
For here in shadows, we'll find a way,
To dance with night until the day.

Whispers of the Celestial Stage

On the stage where stars align,
Whispers fade, but truths entwine.
Celestial tales unfold in space,
Glimmers of light, a cosmic grace.

Every heartbeat tells a story,
Of ancient love and fleeting glory.
In the silence, echoes reign,
Binding us in joy and pain.

As constellations twist and twirl,
We find our place in this vast swirl.
With every star, a wish takes flight,
Illuminated in the velvet night.

Join the dance of fate's embrace,
In the glow, we find our place.
For on this stage, we all belong,
In whispers soft, we sing our song.

Sorcery in the Shadows

In the quiet of the night,
Whispers float, taking flight.
Mysteries dance, shadows play,
Secrets linger, drift away.

Cloaked in darkness, spells are spun,
Underneath the silvered sun.
Magic weaves through the air,
Concealed wonders, everywhere.

Potions brew in hidden nooks,
Silent echoes, ancient books.
A flicker of light, a glint of hope,
In the shadows, dreams elope.

Enchantments weave a delicate thread,
With every heartbeat, life is fed.
Sorcery thrives where few may tread,
In the twilight, magic is spread.

Fantasia in Midnight Hues

Beneath the stars, colors bloom,
A canvas vast, dispelling gloom.
Each shade whispers tales untold,
Fantasia's magic, vibrant and bold.

Moonlight dances on the sea,
Painting dreams, setting them free.
In the quiet, stories blend,
Midnight hues that never end.

Crimson, violet, azure bright,
The realm unfolds, pure delight.
With every breath, we take a chance,
In this world, we find our dance.

Softly woven, threads of night,
Canvas of wonder, purest light.
In the silence, hearts will fuse,
Creating life in midnight hues.

Threads of Enchantment

A tapestry of whispered dreams,
Stitched with care, unraveling seams.
Golden threads in twilight spun,
Each knot a tale, begun and done.

In the quiet, secrets twine,
Binding hearts with threads divine.
A shimmering web, fragile yet strong,
In this dance, we all belong.

Through the ages, stories flow,
In every stitch, the magic grows.
Interwoven, destinies trace,
Threads of enchantment weave our grace.

Embrace the patterns, bold and bright,
Illuminate the darkest night.
In every fiber, life's sweet song,
A symphony where we belong.

A Journey Through the Veil

Beyond the mist, a world awaits,
Hidden paths, intertwined fates.
Step softly through the midnight gray,
A journey starts to lead the way.

Veils of time and shimmering light,
Guide the lost into the night.
With every heartbeat, souls align,
In this realm, the stars will shine.

Mysterious whispers guide our feet,
In this realm, where dreams compete.
Echoes of laughter, shadows bloom,
Filling the air with sweet perfume.

Hold your breath, the magic calls,
In the silence, wonder falls.
Through the veil, we find our way,
A journey crafted, night or day.

Shadows of Whispers

In the twilight, shadows dance,
Softly weaving in a trance.
Secrets murmur, echoes fade,
Lost in dreams that time has made.

Silhouettes of fleeting sighs,
Underneath the starlit skies.
Whispers linger, shadows twine,
Carrying tales that intertwine.

Merriment in the Moonbeams

Glowing light on silver beams,
Dancing hearts weave gossamer dreams.
With laughter sweet, the night ignites,
A symphony of pure delights.

In the glow where shadows play,
Joyful spirits come to stay.
Underneath the moon's soft gaze,
Time dissolves in radiant haze.

Secrets of the Silent Night

Stars confide in hushed tones,
Secrets whispered, old as stones.
In the calm, the world unwinds,
Silence speaks, the heart reminds.

Dreams take flight on gentle breeze,
Boundless thoughts, as slow-time flees.
Beneath the cloak of deep embrace,
Soft reflections find their place.

The Spellbinder's Embrace

With a touch, the spell is cast,
Moments gathered from the past.
In the stillness, magic stirs,
Mysteries in golden furs.

Eyes like lanterns, warm and bright,
Guide us through the outstretched night.
In the shadows, dreams take flight,
Binding souls with pure delight.

Whirlwind of Whimsy

Dancing leaves in playful breeze,
Echoes of laughter in the trees.
Colors twirl in vibrant flight,
A joyful scene, pure delight.

Clouds of candy, skies of cheer,
Whispers of dreams that draw us near.
In this realm where spirits soar,
Imagination opens door.

Chasing shadows, fleeting light,
Moments captured, sweet and bright.
A symphony of hearts entwined,
In this whimsy, joy we find.

Every turn, a new surprise,
Magic sparkles in our eyes.
In this whirlwind, spirits run,
Embrace the chaos, join the fun.

Unseen Wonders at Dusk

Shadows lengthen, night descends,
Whispers of secrets, time suspends.
Stars awaken, glittering bright,
Painting stories across the night.

Crickets sing a lullaby,
Moonlight dances, soft and sly.
In hidden corners, wonders wait,
Nature's magic, small and great.

The world transforms, a mystical veil,
Faintest glow on a winding trail.
Unseen wonders in the dark,
Silhouette of dreams, a spark.

Mysterious paths, a soft embrace,
Every heartbeat finds its place.
In the stillness, spirits gleam,
Dusk reveals the hidden dream.

The Curiosity Cabinet

A door creaks, the world inside,
Artifacts where wonders bide.
Trinkets whisper tales of yore,
Each a glimpse, a secret door.

Feathers, stones, and ancient shells,
In quiet corners, magic dwells.
Every object holds a tale,
In the silence, echoes sail.

Curious eyes explore with glee,
In this realm, hearts roam free.
Dusty memories intertwine,
Stories captured in this shrine.

A treasure trove of thoughts and dreams,
Find the truth in thrill of schemes.
In this cabinet, time stands still,
Curiosity's endless thrill.

A Canvas of Cosmic Mirage

Brush strokes meld in hues profound,
Galaxies swirl, a visual sound.
Nebulas bloom in vibrant flare,
Artistry of the cosmic air.

Stars collide, in splendor collide,
Painting chaos with cosmic pride.
Whispers travel from afar,
Cascading light of every star.

Infinite canvas stretched wide,
Imagination is our guide.
Each brush reveals a universe,
In every stroke, we gently traverse.

A mirage floats, soft and grand,
Visions cradle in time's hand.
In this cosmos, dreams align,
A masterpiece of the divine.

Moonlit Sorcery Unveiled

In the glow of night, magic stirs,
Whispers dance on the silken air,
Mysteries wrapped in silver fur,
Secrets linger, fragile, rare.

Stars twinkle like eyes in the dark,
Casting dreams upon the glade,
Wands held high, igniting a spark,
Ancient spells in moonbeams made.

Beneath the veil, enchantments bloom,
Each shadow a tale to unfold,
In this realm where wonders loom,
Night's embrace, both fierce and bold.

Sorcery swirls in twilight's grace,
Awakening hearts to the call,
Under the moon's ethereal lace,
Together, we rise, destined to fall.

The Timekeeper's Trials

Ticking clocks through the ages run,
A keeper stands, with wisdom vast,
Guarding moments, lost and won,
Choices made echo in the past.

Through the sands of time, he weaves,
Threads of fate both heavy and light,
Each decision, the heart believes,
Moments lost in endless flight.

Count the beats of hearts in sorrow,
While laughter sings in fleeting days,
Lessons learned shape a new tomorrow,
In the balance, life's twisted ways.

The trials faced, both dark and bright,
Echo a journey, long and wide,
In every tick, a spark of light,
In time's embrace, we learn to bide.

Twilight's Hidden Wonders

As dusk descends, the colors blend,
Nature whispers as dreams take flight,
In twilight's arms, the day will end,
Magic stirs in the soft twilight.

Creatures of night begin to creep,
Hushed, the world embraces the shade,
Secrets rise from twilight's deep,
A universe quietly made.

Stars awaken, glimmering bright,
Guiding paths in the twilight haze,
Every shadow holds tales of light,
In this hour, let our hearts blaze.

With wonder unveiled at the day's goodbye,
Magic lingers, sweet and tender,
In twilight's embrace, we learn to fly,
Through hidden wonders, we remember.

Chasing Shadows and Stardust

In moonlit whispers, shadows play,
Chasing dreams on a velvet night,
Stardust glimmers, guiding the way,
Hearts ignite with a fevered light.

Every corner holds secrets untold,
Grasping at fragments of time that flee,
Cloaked in night, the spirits unfold,
We chase the echoes, wild and free.

Through the darkness, our laughter rings,
Bright as the stars in a sea of black,
Hope entwined with the joy time brings,
With every step, there's no looking back.

As dawn approaches, shadows recede,
Yet the stardust remains in our souls,
Chasing dreams, hearts plant a seed,
In the night's embrace, we find our roles.

A Troupe of Night's Wonders

In shadows deep, the figures sway,
A dance unseen, they weave and play.
With whispered dreams in silent night,
They bring to life the stars' soft light.

Through the moonlight, their secrets glide,
A tapestry of fate and pride.
Each twirl a tale of yore and grace,
In this enchanted, hidden space.

The air is thick with magic's call,
As stardust drifts and echoes fall.
They spin the night in vibrant hues,
A spectacle, the heart renews.

With every step, a story's spun,
Until the rise of morning sun.
The troupe will vanish, lost in dreams,
Leaving behind the night's soft gleams.

Dusk's Captivating Charade

As twilight casts its velvet shroud,
The world grows soft, and whispers loud.
A dance of shadows, secrets spun,
Dusk's canvas painted, day is done.

The silhouettes in colors blend,
Each darkened hue, a message send.
They twirl and leap, a playful game,
In dusk's embrace, none are the same.

With fleeting glances, starlight glows,
Awakening dreams in twilight's throes.
Laughter echoes, soft and sweet,
In this charade, where hearts do meet.

When night descends, the curtain falls,
The day retreats, the night enthralls.
Dusk will return, as rules of fate,
In whispered calm, we celebrate.

The Stardust Performance

On cosmic stage, the night unfolds,
A story bright, in starlight told.
With every twinkle, tales arise,
In stardust dreams beneath the skies.

The galaxies spin in rhythmic grace,
As comets dash, they weave and chase.
Each glimmer shines with ancient lore,
A dance of hopes, forevermore.

In quiet awe, the world will stand,
As constellations take command.
They guide the eyes to see beyond,
In endless space, we're not yet gone.

With open hearts, we cast our sights,
To follow paths of wondrous nights.
The stars perform, our spirits rise,
In the embrace of vast, dark skies.

Illumination of the Enigmas

In midnight's realm, the questions dwell,
Wrapped in shadows, stories swell.
With every flicker, truths emerge,
In whispered thoughts, we start to surge.

The moonlight dances on hidden trails,
As mystic winds tell woven tales.
In riddles spun through time and space,
We find the answers we must chase.

With eyes wide open, hearts prepare,
To face the enigmas lurking there.
Each star a guide, a beacon bright,
Illuminating the endless night.

So take my hand, let's wander far,
Through paths of wonder, guided by star.
In this dark dance, we will find light,
Illumination of the night's plight.

Mirrors of Imagination

In reflections deep and wide,
Dreams and shadows often hide.
With each glance, a story spins,
A world where every heart begins.

Colors dance and visions weave,
What to keep and what to leave.
Caught between what's real and dream,
Life is more than what it seems.

Voices echo, soft and clear,
Each whisper draws us ever near.
In the mirror's gaze we find,
The magic of the heart and mind.

Time will bend, and space will shift,
In imagination, we can lift.
So close your eyes and let it play,
In mirrors' depths, we'll find our way.

Allure of the Abyss

Deep below, where silence reigns,
The ocean holds its dark remains.
A call that lures with whispers low,
Into the depths, we long to go.

Shadows swim and secrets sleep,
In hidden caves, the waters creep.
Mysteries dance in currents bold,
Tales of wonders yet untold.

The allure pulls with magic's thread,
To places where the brave have tread.
But is the journey worth the fall,
When darkness answers every call?

Yet in the depths, a light may gleam,
A chance to chase the fleeting dream.
The abyss hums a haunting tune,
Of lost desires, beneath the moon.

Charmers in the Gloom

In corners where the shadows play,
The charmers weave their sly ballet.
With gentle smiles and winking eyes,
They turn the night to sweet surprise.

Flickering candles cast their light,
On faces dancing through the night.
In the gloom, their laughter sings,
Of hidden joys and secret things.

Each whispered word, a velvet thread,
A tapestry of dreams once said.
They draw us close with gentle grace,
And in that moment, time's erased.

Beware the spell that they can cast,
For charmers know the die is cast.
In the embrace of midnight's bloom,
We lose ourselves within the gloom.

Phantoms of the Spotlight

When the lights dim and shadows blend,
The phantoms come and softly wend.
In every corner, secrets lie,
Beneath the stage where dreams can fly.

They dance in whispers, faint and low,
Echoes of those who used to show.
With every step, a tale unfolds,
Of glories past and hearts so bold.

The crowd roars loud, but do they see,
The souls who haunt the melody?
Stars that shone and fell away,
Lost in the night, where they can't stay.

Yet in the silence, there's a breath,
A life once lived, a silent death.
Phantoms linger where dreams ignite,
In shadows cast by fleeting light.

Midnight's Resplendent Riddle

In the hush of night, whispers sing,
Stars unveil secrets, soft as spring.
Moonlit paths where shadows dance,
Heartbeats echo in a trance.

Veils of silver, woven tight,
Mysteries unfold, cloaked in light.
Each twinkle holds a tale untold,
In dreams remembered, brave and bold.

Through the mist, a lantern glows,
Guiding souls where the silence flows.
Curiosity swells like the tide,
In midnight's magic, we confide.

A riddle whispered on the breeze,
Teasing hearts with playful ease.
Unlocking wonders in the night,
Midnight's riddle, pure delight.

The Sorcerer's Veil

In shadows deep, the sorcerer waits,
Casting spells that twist our fates.
Veil of silence, secrets spun,
The world awakes, its journey begun.

Wands of willow, words like fire,
Unraveling dreams, lifting higher.
Mystic runes on ancient stone,
Chanting truths that chill to the bone.

With a flick of wrist, he changes time,
Blurring lines of reason and rhyme.
In the twilight where magic thrives,
The sorcerer's wisdom, it drives.

Behind the veil, past shadows cast,
Lies a future forged from the past.
With each incantation, fate is sealed,
In the sorcerer's veil, truth revealed.

Chimeras in the Twilight

In twilight's grasp, the chimeras roam,
Whispers of fantasy, far from home.
Wings of gossamer, tails of flame,
Creatures of night, wild and untame.

They dance in circles, creating dreams,
Moonlight weaves magic in silver streams.
Eyes aglow with secrets deep,
Guardians of wonders, awake from sleep.

Fables of old breathe life anew,
Chimeras stirring, elusive and true.
Through thickets and shadows, they glide,
In twilight's embrace, dreams can't hide.

With every heartbeat, they draw near,
In enchanting twilight, free from fear.
Chimeras beckon, a call unconfined,
To fly through the dusk, our souls entwined.

Kaleidoscope of Dreams

In a kaleidoscope of vibrant hues,
Dreams intertwine, inviting views.
Fragments of laughter, whispers of hope,
Weaving a tapestry, learning to cope.

Each turn reveals a different light,
Shifting patterns, day into night.
Colors cascading like flowing streams,
Flashes of joy, echoes of dreams.

In this mosaic, we find our way,
Through the labyrinth of night and day.
Glimmers of wisdom interlace,
In the dreams we chase, we find our place.

With open hearts and minds that soar,
Kaleidoscope visions, forever explore.
In every shade, a story told,
In dreams embraced, our spirits unfold.

Night's Grand Transformation

The sun dips low, a fading light,
As shadows blend with coming night.
Stars awaken, pure and bright,
Whispers call, a soft delight.

The moon ascends, a silver queen,
Casting dreams where none have been.
The world beneath in silence hums,
As magic stirs and softly comes.

In darkened woods, the secrets dwell,
With stories only night can tell.
Each rustle brings a hidden glance,
Inviting hearts to dream and dance.

So breathe it in, this twilight air,
As wonders float, beyond compare.
In night's embrace, all souls take flight,
In the calm of night, a sweet respite.

Enigma of the Ethereal

In misty realms where shadows play,
An ethereal dance of night and day.
Wisps of light, a fleeting sigh,
Mysteries weave beneath the sky.

The stars conspire, a twinkling throng,
In cosmic tales where dreams belong.
Whispers trace the ancient lore,
In silence bound, forevermore.

As veils lift softly, visions bloom,
In sacred spaces, darkness looms.
The heart of night conceals its grace,
Embracing each celestial place.

Lost in wonder, beneath the glow,
The soul unravels, free to flow.
In this enigma, time stands still,
As the universe bends to will.

Rapture in the Nocturnal

When twilight falls, a hush descends,
The world transforms, as night transcends.
Beneath the stars, our spirits lift,
In rapture born of night's sweet gift.

The moonlight dances on the streams,
Igniting all forgotten dreams.
Each breath we take, a sigh of bliss,
In shadows deep, we steal a kiss.

Across the fields, the nightingale,
Sings soft and sweet, a haunting tale.
With every note, our hearts entwine,
In this nocturnal, sacred shrine.

In the embrace of shadows' art,
We find a place to mend the heart.
Through night's allure, we feel the rush,
In perfect stillness, love's sweet hush.

Glimmers of Sorcery

In hidden glades, where starlight sways,
Glimmers of sorcery weave their ways.
Crimson threads of twilight glow,
Dancing lightly, swift and slow.

The air is thick with ancient charms,
Drawing souls with unseen arms.
Mystical whispers fill the night,
As magic flares in soft twilight.

From deep within, the shadows breathe,
Revealing secrets few believe.
In every spark, a tale begins,
A world transformed, where wonder spins.

So let us roam under the sky,
Where dreams take flight, and phantoms fly.
In glimmers cast by night's attire,
We find the magic that we desire.

Alchemy of the Night

Stars wink lightly in the dark,
Whispers weave through ancient trees,
Moonlight spills like liquid gold,
Embracing shadows, gentle breeze.

A potion brewed, unseen delights,
Dreams are mixed beneath the sky,
Secrets swirl in twilight's arms,
As silence sings, and phantoms fly.

Crimson petals on the ground,
Echoes of a time long past,
Mysteries of the hidden world,
In twilight's glow, they hold steadfast.

The night unfolds its velvet cloak,
Embracing all, both wild and meek,
In every heart, a spark remains,
A dance of light we dare to seek.

The Scribe of Sorcery

Ink flows freely on the page,
Chanting spells with every stroke,
Ancient runes start to come alive,
In shadows deep, the magic spoke.

Quills that trace the lines of fate,
Binding worlds with written lore,
Each tale spun with care and grace,
Unlocks the door to ancient more.

The scribe knows secrets deep and wide,
Guarded truths in whispered tones,
History etched in ink and fire,
Of heroes lost and timeless thrones.

With every word, a tale unfurls,
Entwined with dreams and destinies,
Through parchment thin, enchantments breathe,
A world awakened with ease.

The Enchantress's Call

In twilight's hue, her voice so sweet,
A melody that stirs the heart,
She calls the stars to dance and spin,
In dreams of night, we shall not part.

With every whisper, shadows play,
Casting spells both soft and light,
Her laughter floats on silken strands,
Entwining souls in velvet night.

A touch of grace, a clasp of hands,
The air ignites with tender fire,
Her gaze, a promise whispered low,
Igniting all our wildest desire.

In every glance, enchantments weave,
Binding us in magic's thrall,
As long as night's embrace remains,
We follow her, the enchantress's call.

Dance of the Enigmatic

In moonlit glades where shadows twine,
The mystics waltz through modern dreams,
Whirling secrets wrapped in light,
In the silence, destiny gleams.

Figures dart with fleeting grace,
Eclipses bend the line of time,
With every step a story told,
In rhythms steeped in hidden rhyme.

Their eyes aglow with ancient fire,
Dance to tunes of suns long dimmed,
The echoes of forgotten stars,
In this embrace, our hearts are brimmed.

So let us join the endless tide,
In the dance of the enigmatic flow,
For in this night, we find our truth,
As the stars above begin to glow.

Spellbound in the Stillness

In the hush of the night, whispers cling,
Stars above like silver blades swing.
Moonlight drapes its soft embrace,
Time slows down in this sacred space.

Crickets sing their gentle tune,
Dreams awaken beneath the moon.
Shadows dance on the forest floor,
Nature's secrets, forevermore.

Breathless moments, hearts entwined,
In this stillness, all is aligned.
Every heartbeat feels so surreal,
Lost in the magic, we cannot conceal.

The world fades away, just us two,
Spellbound in silence, all feels true.
In the calm, we find our way,
In the stillness, we wish to stay.

The Dreamweaver's Dance

In slumber's grip, the dreamer twirls,
Where time is lost and magic unfurls.
With every step, the shadows shift,
In realms unseen, her spirits lift.

Threads of silver, threads of gold,
Weaving stories yet untold.
With every twirl, new visions wake,
A tapestry of dreams she'll make.

Stars align in a lover's sigh,
Whispers of wind, a lullaby.
As dawn approaches, dreams will fade,
But in her heart, the dance won't jade.

Hand in hand with the moonlit night,
She'll chase the dreams till morning light.
In every dip, in every prance,
The world feels right, the dreamer's dance.

A Night of Enigmas

Underneath a veil of dark,
Secrets whisper, mysteries spark.
The moon wears a cloak of silver mist,
In shadows deep, dreams persist.

Footsteps echo on cobbled streets,
Each corner hides untold feats.
Beneath the stars, stories unfurl,
Wonders awaken in this twirling world.

Eyes like lanterns in the dim,
Reflecting tales, both bold and grim.
As night unfolds its curious guise,
We search for truth in hidden lies.

Moments linger, forever bound,
In the silence, enigma's sound.
As whispers fade with the dawn's first light,
We carry the night, wrapped in its fright.

Twilight's Tapestry Unfurled

When day surrenders to evening's call,
Hues of orange and purple enthrall.
Threads of twilight weave through the trees,
A canvas painted by dusk's soft breeze.

The sky whispers secrets, soft and rare,
As shadows dance in the cool night air.
Crickets chirp a lullaby sweet,
In every corner, the heart skips a beat.

Fingers of light stretch gently to touch,
Moments like these, we cherish so much.
With every sigh, the world falls away,
As stars emerge, bidding farewell to the day.

In twilight's glow, we find our place,
A refuge wrapped in nature's grace.
With soft embraces, we follow the way,
Through twilight's tapestry, night claims the day.

Twilight's Spell Weaver

Beneath the sky's soft glow,
Whispers dance in air,
Shadows weave their dreams,
In twilight's gentle stare.

Stars begin to twinkle,
As day starts to fade,
Night's embrace grows tender,
In magic's cloak arrayed.

The moon, a silver sentinel,
Guides the wayward hearts,
With every glimmer, secrets,
From dusk, a world departs.

In this enchanted hour,
Lost souls find their way,
Twilight's spell everlasting,
As night engulfs the day.

Allure of the Invisible

In shadows softly hiding,
Whispers call to me,
The unseen pulls my spirit,
In realms of mystery.

Beneath the veil of silence,
A presence lingers near,
The heartbeats of the hidden,
Resound for those who hear.

Fragments of the unknown,
Glimmer in the night,
They beckon with their promise,
Of love and truth in flight.

In every silent moment,
There's magic in the air,
The allure of the invisible,
A mystery laid bare.

Cosmos and Conjuration

Galaxies in motion,
A dance of pure delight,
The cosmos spins its tales,
In the velvet night.

Stars whisper incantations,
With wishes on their breath,
Each shimmer a reminder,
Of hope that knows no death.

We weave our dreams with starlight,
Conjuring the vast,
Through cosmic threads so timeless,
Our futures are recast.

In the silence of the universe,
We grasp at what we seek,
With every wish a journey,
The stars, our guides unique.

Fables of the Luminous Dark

In darkness lies a story,
Of creatures soft and bright,
They glow with ancient wisdom,
A beacon in the night.

Fables spun from shadows,
Both tender and profound,
In every whispered secret,
A treasure to be found.

The luminous embrace of night,
Casts away all fears,
With every flash of starlight,
A river of our tears.

Through the tapestry of twilight,
Truths and legends blend,
In the fables of the luminous dark,
Where dreams and realities mend.

Glittering Dreams in Twilight

In the dusk where shadows play,
Whispers of the night sway.
Stars ignite the velvet sky,
Dreams take flight, they soar and fly.

Colors blend in twilight's glow,
Mysteries begin to flow.
Laughter dances on soft air,
In this realm, we shed our care.

Echoes of a fleeting song,
Guide our hearts where we belong.
Gentle breezes brush our skin,
In this moment, we begin.

Let the dreams in twilight gleam,
Sparkling bright like every dream.
Hold them close, let magic rise,
Beneath the vast and starlit skies.

Phantoms of Illusion

In the maze of mists we tread,
Figures shift, and fears are fed.
Echoes whisper, shadows sigh,
Fleeting forms that drift on by.

Illusions dance on realms unseen,
Veils of truth and light between.
Caught in webs of dreams we weave,
In these phantoms, we believe.

Shapes that flicker, memories lost,
In the dance, we count the cost.
Ghostly trails lead us astray,
Yet in the dark, we find our way.

From illusions, we may see,
The hidden truths that whisper free.
Phantoms guide with subtle winks,
Inviting thoughts as the heart thinks.

The Whispering Masquerade

Behind the masks, where secrets bide,
A world of dreams and sins collide.
Laughter mingles, joy and pain,
In this masquerade, we gain.

Faces change like flowing streams,
Fleeting glimpses of our dreams.
Veils of silk and lace entwine,
In this dance, our hearts align.

Whispers float on velvet night,
Hidden truths twinkle bright.
Every mask a story told,
In the dark, we're brave and bold.

Let the masquerade unfold,
In the night, our hearts consoled.
With every glance, we dare to see,
The whispering truth that sets us free.

Midnight's Call to Wonder

At midnight's stroke, a world awakes,
With every dream that softly breaks.
Stars descend, a cloak of light,
Calling souls into the night.

Cloaked in magic, shadows sway,
Guiding hearts that drift away.
Curiosity ignites the air,
Inviting all to dream and dare.

With every breath, the world expands,
Magic stirs in unseen hands.
Midnight's call, a secret song,
Pulls us close, we all belong.

In the stillness, wonders gleam,
Awakening each whispered dream.
Let the night be our wild guide,
In midnight's arms, we will abide.

Enigmas Wrapped in Night

Whispers weave in shadows deep,
Mysteries that silence keep.
Stars like secrets, softly glow,
Dancing where the night winds blow.

Veils of dusk enfold the light,
Truth concealed from curious sight.
Each gaze casts a spell so pure,
Searching for what's yet unsure.

In the stillness, echoes call,
Promises that linger, enthrall.
As the moon begins to rise,
Shaping dreams from whispered sighs.

Hearts enshrouded in the dark,
In shadows lies the hidden spark.
Wrapped in enigmas, we find grace,
Embracing all that time can trace.

An Evening of Bewitchment

Beneath the twilight's soft embrace,
Magic dances, time and space.
Candles flicker, shadows play,
Enchantments fill the air this day.

Whirling leaves, a charming tune,
Moonlight sprinkles like a boon.
In the stillness, passions bloom,
Hearts entwined within the gloom.

Waves of laughter, whispers sweet,
Every heartbeat feels the heat.
Underneath the starry sky,
Weaving dreams as hours fly.

A tapestry of night unfurls,
In the magic, love twirls.
An evening framed by mystic light,
Forever marked, an endless flight.

Echoes of Enchantment

In the twilight, stories weave,
Echoes call, yet none believe.
Chasing shadows, time stands still,
Whispers promise secret thrill.

Winds of night, a gentle sigh,
Carry tales that haunt the sky.
Through the trees, a laugh cascades,
Memories in silence wades.

Footsteps trace the hidden paths,
Where the starlight feels the wrath.
Glimmers twinkle, hope ignites,
In the depths of starry nights.

Each moment drips like silver rain,
Softly cleansing every pain.
In the echoes, dreams are spun,
Enchanted hearts eternally run.

Starlight Underneath the Cloak

Cloaked in night, we seek the dawn,
Starlit whispers gently drawn.
Every twinkle tells a tale,
Wrapped in dreams that softly sail.

Beneath the cloak, the world sleeps,
In the stillness, magic peeps.
Veils of darkness cradle hope,
Guiding souls to learn to cope.

Moonbeams brush the earth so light,
Tales of love and depth ignite.
In this space, vast and wide,
Hearts awaken, dreams collide.

Underneath the shroud of time,
We find solace in the rhyme.
Starlight beckons on the way,
Showing paths where spirits play.

Tides of Twilight

The sun dips low, a golden sigh,
Whispers of day begin to die.
Colors blend in a soft embrace,
Time slows down, in this sacred space.

Gentle waves caress the shore,
As night unfurls its velvet lore.
Stars awaken, one by one,
In the afterglow of the setting sun.

Clouds drift by, a silken stream,
Moonlight dances, a waking dream.
Shadows stretch, a playful tease,
In the twilight's gentle breeze.

With every breath, the magic grows,
A tranquil hush, the heart knows.
Nature's canvas, vast and wide,
In the hush of twilight, we confide.

Glistening Spells in the Mist

Mystic shrouds veil the ground,
Where secrets of nature abound.
Each droplet glimmers, a tiny star,
Casting spells from near and far.

Silence weaves through the tall trees,
As whispers ride on the gentle breeze.
Veils of vapor, soft and light,
In the heart of the misty night.

Elusive shadows start to play,
In the silver dawn of a brand new day.
Nature's magic, pure and sweet,
In every corner, feel the beat.

With each step, the world will shift,
In glistening spells, find your gift.
Through fog and dream, let your heart roam,
In the mist, you are never alone.

Luminescent Echoes of the Night

Stars flicker in the vast dark sea,
Whispering tales of eternity.
Moonbeams glint on water's face,
Carrying dreams to a distant place.

Softly hums the nightingale's song,
A melody to which we belong.
Glistening echoes, long and deep,
In the silence, the world will sleep.

Each constellation, a story told,
In the night, the brave and bold.
Awakening hearts to seek the light,
In the wondrous depths of night.

Luminous whispers guide our way,
Through shadowed paths where spirits sway.
In every echo, a spark ignites,
Illuminating the vast delights.

Gossamer Threads of Wonder

In the dawn, where shadows weave,
Gossamer threads of dreams conceive.
Delicate patterns, soft and bright,
Woven together, a wondrous sight.

Nature's fabric, rich and rare,
Each thread whispers, beyond compare.
A tapestry of joys and fears,
Stitched tightly by the passing years.

In every wrinkle, a tale resides,
Of love, loss, and the ebbing tides.
Through light and dark, the stories blend,
A journey that will never end.

So pause and admire the threads of fate,
In gossamer beauty, we celebrate.
For in each moment, we come to see,
The wonderous web of life's decree.

An Odyssey in Obscurity

In shadows deep, we wander slow,
Through pathways dim where secrets flow.
Each step a tale, unheard, unseen,
An odyssey where dreams convene.

The stars above, they pulse and gleam,
Illuminating what we deem.
We chase the whispers of the night,
In search of truths both bold and slight.

With every turn, we find our fate,
In hidden doors we contemplate.
The mystery calls, a haunting song,
In obscurity, we all belong.

So let us dance in twilight's grace,
Embrace the dark, our secret place.
For in this journey, we will find,
The light and shadows intertwined.

The Ethereal Performance

A stage set high in realms above,
With echoes sweet of songs we love.
The dancers twirl in silken threads,
Their movements speak where silence treads.

Each note a brush upon the air,
Creating dreams that we all share.
In moonlit glow, the curtain sways,
Unveiling heartbeats, lost in praise.

The audience, with bated breath,
Awaits the magic, hints of death.
A performance rich with life's embrace,
Where time dissolves in art's soft grace.

As shadows fade, the echoes soar,
In every soul, a yearning roar.
For in this space, we truly live,
In ethereal moments, love we give.

Enchanted Horizons Await

As dawn breaks bright, a promise calls,
To lands where wonder gently falls.
The skies unfurl, a canvas wide,
Where dreams and hopes are woven, tied.

With every step on emerald fields,
The heart unveils what joy reveals.
Mountains rise with a whispered plea,
Enchanted horizons set us free.

The rivers dance in sunlight's grace,
Reflecting smiles on nature's face.
In every corner, magic grows,
In every heartbeat, passion flows.

So take my hand, let's journey far,
To places penned by every star.
For in this quest, our spirits heighten,
In enchanted realms, our hearts brighten.

Light Beneath the Cloak

In twilight's hush, a secret glows,
A gentle warmth that softly shows.
Beneath the cloak of night's embrace,
There lies a light, a sacred space.

With every shadow, dreams arise,
In whispered thoughts, a soft surprise.
The glow reveals what's lost and found,
In stillness deep, our hearts resound.

Across the dark, a pathway gleams,
Illuminating all our dreams.
With courage born from hidden grace,
We step towards the light's embrace.

So let the night, with all its charms,
Wrap us close in its tender arms.
For in this cloak, we come to see,
The light within, our destiny.

Phantom Lights Dancing

In the hush of twilight's glow,
Shadows twist and softly flow.
Glimmers whisper of the night,
Phantom lights take graceful flight.

Through the trees, they weave and sway,
Chasing dreams that drift away.
A ballet in the starry air,
Specters waltz without a care.

Mystic glows paint the dark,
Each flicker a secret spark.
Dancing like forgotten tunes,
Underneath the watchful moons.

When dawn arrives, they fade from sight,
Leaving echoes of delight.
Yet in hearts they leave a trace,
Phantom lights, a soft embrace.

Conjuror of the Night Sky

In the depths of endless night,
Stars awaken, shining bright.
Whispers woven in the air,
Conjuror of dreams laid bare.

With a flick, the heavens spin,
Casting spells where time begins.
Underneath the cosmic glow,
Magic dances, free to flow.

Celestial hands caress the dark,
Sparking worlds with just a spark.
Galaxies twirl in a ballet,
Guided by the night's soft sway.

Every twinkle tells a tale,
Of the wanderers who set sail.
In the silence, wisdom grows,
Conjuror's art, the heart bestows.

Beyond the Velvet Curtain

A tapestry of night unfolds,
Lush and deep, with stories told.
Velvet drapes conceal the light,
Mysteries of the coming night.

Fingers trace the fabric's weave,
Secrets lingering, we believe.
Twilight hints at dreams untied,
Veils of shadows gently bide.

Step into the dreams that call,
Beyond the curtain's tender thrall.
Whispered hopes, the stars embrace,
In the quiet, find your place.

For in the depth of every seam,
Lies the comfort of a dream.
Beyond the velvet, worlds await,
Open the door, don't hesitate.

Mysteries in the Moonbeams

Softly spills the silver light,
Moonbeams dance throughout the night.
Casting shadows, wise and deep,
Holding secrets while we sleep.

Cascades of whispers fill the air,
Every shimmer, a gentle prayer.
For in the glow, stories weave,
Of lost hopes and dreams we grieve.

Midnight magic starts to play,
Heartfelt wishes drift away.
Each soft ray a guiding star,
Leading souls, no matter how far.

So let the moonbeams kiss your skin,
Awakening the dreams within.
For in their light, we find the way,
Mysteries that softly stay.

Mirage in the Moonlight

In the stillness of night, shadows weave,
A dance of whispers, hearts believe.
The moon casts dreams on silken streams,
Echoes of wishes, glittering beams.

A soft breeze stirs the silvery light,
Guiding lost souls in flight.
Reflections shimmer, illusions play,
In the mirage, we drift away.

Stars wink softly, secrets unfold,
As stories of lovers are gently told.
With every glance, the world seems right,
A fairytale born in the moon's sweet light.

So linger where the shadows dance,
Embrace the magic, take a chance.
In the mirage, let your heart soar,
For in the moonlight, we are evermore.

Every Flicker Tells a Story

In the hearth's glow, memories spin,
Flickering flames where tales begin.
Whispers of yesterdays softly rise,
In every spark, a truth to disguise.

Candles flicker, shadows play,
Painting dreams in night's ballet.
Each light a portal, a moment in time,
Every flicker preserved in rhyme.

From happy laughter to sorrowful sighs,
The flames record love and goodbyes.
Each flicker holds dreams yet untold,
A tapestry rich, a story bold.

So gather 'round, let the stories flow,
In the flickering light, let your heart know.
For every flame and every glow,
Holds a piece of life, a life we sow.

Secrets of the Enigmatic Night

Under a veil of twinkling stars,
The night whispers secrets from afar.
In shadows deep, mysteries play,
Guarding the thoughts we dare not say.

Each gust of wind, a voice unheard,
Carrying whispers, a lover's word.
The moonlight dances on leaves so bright,
Revealing truths in the heart of night.

In the stillness, silence speaks,
Unraveling stories, the soul it seeks.
Every glance, a knowing spark,
In the intimacy of the dark.

So let your heart open, hear the call,
Secrets of night, enchant us all.
In shadows we wander, hand in hand,
Finding solace in the dreams we've planned.

Echoed Laughter in the Dark

In the quiet corners, laughter waits,
Echoes of joy, the heart celebrates.
Soft giggles linger in moonlit air,
Filling the night, a melody rare.

As shadows dance on the velvet ground,
In whispered secrets, lost souls are found.
Through the darkness, the laughter weaves,
A tapestry of hope that never leaves.

Each chuckle a spark, igniting our souls,
Binding our dreams, making us whole.
In the shadows, shared moments gleam,
Echoed laughter, a night's sweet dream.

So let us wander, hand in hand,
In the dark, where memories stand.
For echoed laughter guides our way,
In the embrace of night, we'll forever stay.

Tricks Under a Shroud of Night

Whispers roam the shadowed streets,
Secrets held where silence meets.
Stars blink down, a watchful eye,
As dreams take flight, the spirits sigh.

Ghostly figures twist and spin,
Chasing echoes, lost within.
Laughter dances with the breeze,
Underneath the ancient trees.

Flickering lights in window panes,
Marking paths of hidden gains.
Each corner turned, a riddle spun,
In the night, all battles won.

Veils of darkness, heavy cloak,
Muffled words, the shadows spoke.
In this realm, we learn to play,
As enchantments guide the way.

Marvels of the Midnight Hour

Strange realms bloom when clock strikes twelve,
Magic stirs, our dreams evolve.
Moonlight paints a shimmering scene,
Unseen wonders, softly gleam.

Whispers echo, secrets shared,
In twilight's embrace, none prepared.
Time stands still, the world a blur,
With every pulse, the night does stir.

Waves of stillness, hearts aglow,
In this haven, lost we go.
Fate's fine threads tightly spun,
As miracles are deftly done.

Underneath the starry dome,
We find a path, a way back home.
Every shadow softly sighs,
In the magic of midnight skies.

Illusions in the Ether

Cascading visions paint the air,
Mysteries wrapped in a gentle flare.
Ethereal trails drift and wane,
Fleeting glimpses, joy and pain.

Colors swirl in silent dance,
Inviting hearts to take a chance.
In the fold of each faint hue,
Worlds emerge, both strange and true.

Echoes murmur from afar,
Guided by a distant star.
Every breath a spell unwinds,
Minding tales of countless kinds.

Reality bends, shapes reform,
Riding winds, we seek the warm.
Each illusion whispers low,
In the ether, dreams will grow.

Fantasies on the Fringe

At the edge where shadows play,
Fantasies chase the light of day.
Fragrant blooms where wild thoughts roam,
In the chaos, we find our home.

The whispering winds tell tales,
Of colorful ships and sunset sails.
Each moment bursts with vibrant flair,
A tapestry woven with care.

Threads of laughter, sighs of hope,
In this space, we freely grope.
Clinging tight to dreams that soar,
On the fringe, we crave for more.

Time may bend, but hearts align,
In this realm, the stars will shine.
Together we navigate the maze,
Lost in the thrill of endless days.

Luminescent Fantasies

In twilight's soft, embracing glow,
Dreams take flight, as feelings flow.
Stars awaken, whispers sing,
Magic dances on silver wing.

Shadows flicker, hopes unite,
Colors blend, a wondrous sight.
The heart ignites, a warm embrace,
Time dissolves in this sacred space.

Echoes linger in the air,
Stories weave without a care.
Each breath taken, dreams unseal,
In luminescent worlds, we feel.

Glimmers fade, but spirits soar,
Chasing luster forevermore.
In fantasies where wishes gleam,
Reality bends to the mind's dream.

The Spellbinding Hour

As twilight drapes a velvet sheet,
Time suspends, a heartbeat sweet.
Magic murmurs through the night,
Whispers soft, encased in light.

Celestial bodies sway above,
Casting spells of endless love.
Moments linger, shadows play,
Enchantment found in night's ballet.

The moonlight spills like liquid gold,
Secrets shared, yet to untold.
Heartbeats fasten, dreams entwine,
In this hour, our souls align.

As dawn approaches, magic wanes,
Yet in our hearts, the love remains.
Forever changed by this embrace,
We hold the hour in a sacred place.

Echoes of the Unseen

In the stillness, whispers call,
Voices rise, yet none stand tall.
Silent songs of hidden grace,
Breathe the thoughts that time erase.

Shadows painted on the wall,
Echoes fade, yet still enthrall.
Memories dance, lost in air,
Unseen paths, our hearts laid bare.

Through the silence, truths align,
In every heartbeat, we define.
The untold stories, soft and clear,
In every echo, love draws near.

We wander through the ghostly night,
With every turn, we chase the light.
Unseen wonders softly gleam,
In the echoes, we find our dream.

Fantasia under the Moon

Beneath the moon's enchanting glow,
A world awakens, spirits flow.
Fantasy drapes the earth in lace,
Dreams ignite in this sacred space.

Winds whisper secrets, soft and light,
Guiding hearts through the velvet night.
Stars twinkle like a lover's sigh,
Painting stories across the sky.

Laughter dances on gossamer breeze,
Every moment invites to seize.
With every heartbeat, magic sways,
Lost in a dance that never decays.

In this fantasia, we find release,
Under the moon, our souls find peace.
A tapestry woven of dreams and light,
Forever cherished in the gentle night.

Between Two Heartbeats

In the quiet, time stands still,
A breath between the moments,
Whispers of a gentle thrill,
Love's pulse, a soft proponent.

Fingers touch like fleeting dreams,
In a world that fades away,
Caught in silken, silver seams,
Here, we linger, lost in sway.

Beneath the stars, we find our way,
Tracing paths of sweet delight,
Every heartbeat, come what may,
Guiding souls into the night.

With every breath, we intertwine,
Echoing the tune of fate,
In a dance that's purely divine,
Two hearts weave the threads of fate.

The Sleight of Hand Reverie

A magician's grace in the night,
Cards flutter like leaves on breeze,
Illusions cast in soft moonlight,
Weaving dreams with practiced ease.

Eyes wide with wondrous surprise,
Secrets linger in the air,
As shadows dance and lovers rise,
Magic flows with tender care.

Time slips through a fragile hand,
Moments vanish into mist,
In this realm, we understand,
Every flick and twist a tryst.

So let us lose ourselves tonight,
In a spell that feels so real,
For in this dream of pure delight,
We find the magic that we feel.

Celestial Carnival

Stars twinkle in a cosmic race,
Galaxies swirl in swirling hues,
The universe a grand embrace,
Painting skies with vibrant clues.

Planets spin in harmony,
A dance of light and shadow bends,
Wonders echo endlessly,
As time and space embrace, transcends.

Comets soar with fiery tails,
Whispers from the great unknown,
In this grand and secret tale,
We find the magic of our own.

Join this dance under the night,
Let your spirit soar and roam,
In the carnival of starlight,
We embrace the cosmos as home.

Night's Mystical Journey

In shadows deep, where dreams are spun,
The night unfolds its velvet wings,
With every step, a journey begun,
As the moonlight softly sings.

The whispering winds, a haunting call,
Guiding hearts through paths unknown,
In the stillness, we feel it all,
The magic in the night is sown.

Stars shimmer like the dreams we chase,
Each one a wish cast to the skies,
In the vastness, we find our place,
A tapestry where hope can rise.

So let us wander hand in hand,
Through night's embrace, we'll roam afar,
In this mystical, enchanted land,
Together, beneath the guiding star.

Whispers of the Darkened Stage

In silence, shadows hold their breath,
As tales unfold, a dance with death.
The curtain sways with secrets deep,
In twilight's grasp, the echoes seep.

The spotlight flickers, hearts ignite,
In whispered tones, they take their flight.
A ghostly voice, a lingering sigh,
Beneath the stars, the dreams reply.

A fleeting glance, a stolen kiss,
In every call, a hint of bliss.
The stage is set, the night is young,
In trembling hearts, the song is sung.

So let the show begin anew,
With whispers shared and memories true.
In darkened halls, our spirits blend,
As dreams take shape, and never end.

Secrets Beneath the Stars

Beneath the canopy of night,
The stars conspire, shining bright.
In shadows cast by ancient trees,
The whispers carry on the breeze.

Each twinkle holds a story told,
Of secrets buried, brave and bold.
A silver thread connects us all,
In silence deep, we heed the call.

The moon, a guardian of our dreams,
Illuminates our quiet schemes.
In starlit paths, we weave our fates,
As twilight wanes, destiny waits.

So trust the magic in the night,
For every secret brings us light.
Beneath the stars, our souls take flight,
And dance together in pure delight.

Enchantment at Hour's End

As daylight dims, the magic stirs,
With twilight's dance, our heartbeats purr.
The world transforms, a pastel hue,
In whispers soft, we find what's true.

The evening calls with velvet grace,
Each moment etched, a warm embrace.
In fading light, our laughter glows,
As time stands still, enchantment flows.

The stars and moon begin their reign,
While shadows weave their sweet refrain.
In every glance, a spark ignites,
As dreams take shape in cozy nights.

So let us linger, hold this spell,
In hour's end, where magic dwells.
With hearts entwined, we make a vow,
To cherish this, the here and now.

Shadows Dance in Moonlight

In silver light, the shadows sway,
As midnight whispers call to play.
With every step, a story spins,
In moonlit glades, the dance begins.

The night enfolds, a soft caress,
With every sigh, we feel the press.
Of gentle dreams in twilight's weave,
As hearts entwine, we dare believe.

A flicker here, a glimmer there,
As dark and light become a pair.
In every turn, a secret we find,
As shadows dance, our souls aligned.

So let us waltz till dawn awakes,
In moonlit moments, love remakes.
With shadows close, we lose the fight,
And find our joy in pure moonlight.

The Illusionist's Lullaby

In shadows cast where secrets twine,
A whisper dances, lost in time.
The stars, they glimmer, softly sway,
As dreams are spun in night's ballet.

A flick of wrist, a fleeting light,
The heartbeats quicken, minds take flight.
With every breath, a tale unfolds,
In twinkling eyes, the magic holds.

The moonlit path, a silent guide,
Where fantasies and truths collide.
With gentle hands, the world transforms,
In every note, a spell that warms.

So close your eyes, let wonders creep,
Into the arms of slumber deep.
For in the dark, the magic lies,
An illusionist beneath the skies.

Dreamcatcher of the Night

Beneath the veil of starry skies,
The dreamcatcher weaves its ties.
A thread of light, a quilt of sound,
In gentle whispers, peace is found.

The moon bestows a silvery glow,
As shadows dance, and breezes blow.
In every hope, a dream takes flight,
Caught in the web of softest night.

The world awakes with sleepy sighs,
While nightingale sings lullabies.
Each echo drifts on velvet air,
A melody of tender care.

So let the dreams within you swell,
Embrace the night, where wishes dwell.
For the dreamcatcher's magic spins,
A tapestry where peace begins.

A Spell in the Stillness

In quiet corners, shadows blend,
Where time suspends and whispers mend.
A stillness falls, a magic brew,
As secrets weave in midnight blue.

The breath of night, a calming tale,
With starlit eyes that softly pale.
Each moment lingers, soft and sweet,
The world recedes, retreating feet.

In silence deep where dreams reside,
A tranquil heart can softly glide.
Through gentle thoughts, a spell is cast,
In stillness found, the die is cast.

So take a breath and feel the glow,
Let worries fade; let calm bestow.
In every heartbeat, peace shall dwell,
A soothing song, a magic spell.

Fantasies in Velvet Curves

In twilight's embrace, dreams softly swirl,
Wrapped in the warmth of a velvet curl.
With whispers sweet, the night unveils,
A tapestry where fantasy sails.

The gentle touch of starlit streams,
Lulls every heart into soft dreams.
With colors bold and shades so bright,
Fantasies bloom in the hush of night.

Through moonlit paths, we wander free,
In secret realms where spirits flee.
Each step adorned in silken grace,
Sparks of wonder in every space.

So close your eyes, let magic weave,
In velvet curves, the heart believes.
For in the dark, where dreams take flight,
Fantasies dance in pure delight.

Milton Keynes UK
Ingram Content Group UK Ltd.
UKHW020735301124
451807UK00019B/794